D0907032

what is this thing called love

Also by Kim Addonizio

The Philosopher's Club

Jimmy & Rita

Tell Me

The Poet's Companion: A Guide to the Pleasures of Writing Poetry (with Dorianne Laux)

In the Box Called Pleasure (Stories)

Dorothy Parker's Elbow: Tattoos on Writers, Writers on Tattoos (edited with Cheryl Dumesnil)

WHAT IS THIS THING
CALLED LOVE

For Allen

6/05
West Chester

kim addonizio

w. w. norton & company   new york london

p. 13: quote used by permission of Ruth Stone /
Yellow Moon Press, story@yellowmoon.com.

For information about permission to reproduce selections from this book,
write to Permissions, W. W. Norton & Company Inc.
500 Fifth Avenue, New York, NY 10110

Manufacturing by Courier Westford
Book design by Blue Shoe Studio
Production manager: Anna Oler

Library of Congress Cataloging-in-Publication Data

Addonizio, Kim, 1954–
What is this thing called love : poems / Kim Addonizio.— 1st ed.
p. cm.
ISBN 0-393-05726-7
I. Title.
PS3551.D3997W48 2004
811'.54—dc22

2003017944

W. W. Norton & Company, Inc.
500 Fifth Avenue, New York, N.Y. 10110
www.wwnorton.com

W. W. Norton & Company Ltd.
Castle House, 75/76 Wells Street, London W1T 3QT

1 2 3 4 5 6 7 8 9 0

For Robert—
lightning twice

CONTENTS

ACKNOWLEDGMENTS ✍❤

Grazie—*for their generous criticism of this manuscript,
and for being my love-dogs: Susan Browne, Cheryl
Dumesnil, Lisa Glatt and David Hernandez, Dorianne
Laux and Joe Millar, Ruth Schwartz. For all their sup-
port: Steve Huff and Thom Ward of BOA Editions.
Much gratitude, for asking: Jill Bialosky. And for being
my corner man, Rob McQuilkin.*

*Grateful acknowledgment is made to the editors of the
following journals where many of these poems were pub-
lished, sometimes in different versions:* American Poetry
Review, Atlanta Review, Bloomsbury Review,
Chelsea, Cimarron Review, Connecticut Review,
Denver Quarterly, Five Points, Iowa Review, Margie,
Pearl, Poetry, Poetry International, Runes, Salt Hill,
Threepenny Review, Water ~ Stone.

*"Miniatures" was awarded first place in the Davoren
Hanna Poetry Competition and first appeared online.*

The wind was shaking me all night long;
shaking me in my sleep
like a definition of love,
saying, this is the moment,
here, now.

        —Ruth Stone, "Green Apples"

The blues are the true facts of life.

         —Willie Dixon

what is this thing called love

ONE

FIRST KISS

Afterwards you had that drunk, drugged look
my daughter used to get, when she had let go
of my nipple, her mouth gone slack and her eyes
turned vague and filmy, as though behind them
the milk was rising up to fill her
whole head, that would loll on the small
white stalk of her neck so I would have to hold her
closer, amazed at the sheer power
of satiety, which was nothing like the needing
to be fed, the wild flailing and crying until she fastened
herself to me and made the seal tight
between us, and sucked, drawing the liquid down and
out of my body; no, *this* was the crowning
moment, this giving of herself, knowing
she could show me how helpless
she was—that's what I saw, that night when you
pulled your mouth from mine and
leaned back against a chain-link fence,
in front of a burned-out church: a man
who was going to be that vulnerable,
that easy and impossible to hurt.

STOLEN MOMENTS

What happened, happened once. So now it's best
in memory—an orange he sliced: the skin
unbroken, then the knife, the chilled wedge
lifted to my mouth, his mouth, the thin
membrane between us, the exquisite orange,
tongue, orange, my nakedness and his,
the way he pushed me up against the fridge—
Now I get to feel his hands again, the kiss
that didn't last, but sent some neural twin
flashing wildly through the cortex. Love's
merciless, the way it travels in
and keeps emitting light. Beside the stove
we ate an orange. And there were purple flowers
on the table. And we still had hours.

BLUES FOR DANTE ALIGHIERI

. . . without hope we live on in desire . . .
                                        Inferno, IV

Our room was too small, the sheets scratchy and hot—
Our room was a kind of hell, we thought,
and killed a half-liter of Drambuie we'd bought.

We walked over the Arno and back across.
We walked all day, and in the evening, lost,
argued and wandered in circles. At last

we found our hotel. The next day we left for Rome.
We found the Intercontinental, and a church full of bones,
and ate takeout Chinese in our suite, alone.

It wasn't a great journey, only a side trip.
It wasn't love for eternity, or any such crap;
it was just something that happened . . .

We packed suitcases, returned the rental car.
We packed souvenirs, repaired to the airport bar
and talked about pornography, and movie stars.

WHAT WAS

The streets fill with cabs and limos,
with the happy laughter of the very drunk;
the benches in Washington Square Park,
briefly occupied by lovers, have been reclaimed

by men who stretch out coughing under the *Chronicle*.
We're sitting on the cold slab
of a cathedral step, and to keep myself
from kissing you I stare at the cartoony

blue neon face of a moose, set over the eponymous
restaurant, and decide on self-pity
as the best solution to this knot
of complicated feelings. So much, my love,

for love; our years together recede,
taillights in the fog that's settled in. I breathe
your familiar smell—Tuscany Per Uomo,
Camel Lights, the sweet reek of alcohol—and keep

from looking at your face, knowing
I'm still a sucker for beauty. Nearby, a man decants

a few notes from his tenor sax, honking his way
through a tune meant to be melancholy. Soon

I'll drive home alone, weeping and raging,
the radio twisted high as I can stand it—
or else I'll lean toward you, and tell you
any lie I think will bring you back.

And if you're reading this, it's been years
since then, and everything's too late
the way it always is in songs like this,
the way it always is.

SO WHAT

Guess what. If love is only chemistry—
phenylethylamine, that molecule
that dizzies up the brain's back room, smoky
with hot bebop, it won't be long until
a single worker's mopping up the scuffed
and littered floor, whistling tunelessly,
each endorphin cooling like a snuffed
glass candle, the air stale with memory.
So what, you say; outside, a shadow lifts
a trumpet from its case, lifts it like an ingot
and scatters a few virtuosic riffs
toward the locked-down stores. You've quit
believing that there's more, but you're still stirred
enough to stop, and wait, listening hard.

31-YEAR-OLD LOVER

When he takes off his clothes
I think of a stick of butter being unwrapped,
the milky, lubricious smoothness of it
when it's taken from the fridge still hard
the way his body is hard, the high
tight pectorals, the new dimes of the nipples pressed
into his chest, the fanning of the muscles underneath.
I look at his arms, shaped as though a knife
has slid along the curves to carve them out,
deltoids, biceps, triceps, I almost can't believe
that he is human—latissimus dorsi, hip flexors,
gluteals, gastrocnemius—he is so perfectly made.
He stands naked in my bedroom and nothing
has harmed him yet, though he is going
to be harmed. He is going to have a gut one day,
and wiry gray hairs where the soft dark filaments
flow out of him, the cream of his skin is going
to loosen and separate slowly, over a low steady flame
and he has no idea, as I had no idea,

and I am not going to speak of this to him ever,

I am going to let him stretch out on my bed

so I can take the heavy richness of him in

and in, I am going to have it back the only way I can.

MUSE

When I walk in,
men buy me drinks before I even reach the bar.

They fall in love with me after one night,
even if we never touch.

I tell you I've got this shit down to a science.

They sweat with my memory,
alone in cheap rooms they listen

to moans through the wall
and wonder if that's me,

letting out a scream as the train whines by.

But I'm already two states away, lying with a boy
I let drink rain from the pulse at my throat.

No one leaves me, I'm the one that chooses.
I show up like money on the sidewalk.

Listen, baby. Those are my high heels dangling from the
    phone wire.

I'm the crow flapping down,
that's my black slip

you catch sight of when the pain
twists into you so deep

you have to close your eyes and weep like a goddamned
    woman.

YOU DON'T KNOW WHAT LOVE IS

but you know how to raise it in me
like a dead girl winched up from a river. How to
wash off the sludge, the stench of our past.
How to start clean. This love even sits up
and blinks; amazed, she takes a few shaky steps.
Any day now she'll try to eat solid food. She'll want
to get into a fast car, one low to the ground, and drive
to some cinderblock shithole in the desert
where she can drink and get sick and then
dance in nothing but her underwear. You know
where she's headed, you know she'll wake up
with an ache she can't locate and no money
and a terrible thirst. So to hell
with your warm hands sliding inside my shirt
and your tongue down my throat
like an oxygen tube. Cover me
in black plastic. Let the mourners through.

BLUES FOR ROBERTO

It's an ugly circus, to leave you again.

It's a carnival act: bound, chained

underwater in a glass tank, near-drowned,

I've gotten free. I'm incredible.

I've gotten so good I'm terrible.

Bring on the elephants, their great legs hobbled.

Bring on a lion, I'll feed it my head.

Bring a small scrap of paper to wipe up the blood.

I'll hang myself from the high wire, nude . . .

Once you loved me, but walked away.

Once was too often, for a girl like me—

Since then I've made you pay and pay.

Don't call me, ever. I'll tell you I'm sorry.

Don't call me, I tell you; it's boring, boring

always to leap to the end of the story.

And this is the end. I'm leaving town.

This is the end: the tents torn down,

the animals making caged animal sounds.

EVER AFTER: A PARADELLE

He lies on his side like a glass knocked over.
He lies on his side like a glass knocked over.
Only a little sweetness left, poor boy.
Only a little sweetness left, poor boy.
Only his little lies, a glass-like sweetness.
Poor he, a left boy knocked over on side.

Now she loves him more, but won't come back.
Now she loves him more, but won't come back.
In dreams she cries and paints his face like a girl's.
In dreams she cries and paints his face like a girl's.
A girl's more in dreams. She won't like him now,
but loves his face. *Come back*, she paints and cries.

It rains and falls dark on the house they lived in together.
It rains and falls dark on the house they lived in together.
She is alone there, afraid when it falls and breaks over the
    roof.
She is alone there, afraid when it falls and breaks over the
    roof.
It is on the roof. Rains and falls. The house afraid
when it lived alone. There she breaks and falls over in dark.

Now, in the dark, he dreams.

She is like a sweetness in his side; she loves him back.

But it paints more lies. Afraid, his face won't come together.

Little boy lived there on and on alone, only a girl's poor roof
knocked over. When it breaks, the house cries like they left.

She rains. And a glass falls and falls.

note: for an explanation of the paradelle form, see Billy Collins's "Paradelle for
Susan" in his book Picnic, Lightning.

SONNENIZIO ON A LINE FROM DRAYTON

Since there's no help, come let us kiss and part;
or kiss anyway, let's start with that, with the kissing part,
because it's better than the parting part, isn't it—-
we're good at kissing, we like how that part goes:
we part our lips, our mouths get near and nearer,
then we're close, my breasts, your chest, our bodies partway
to making love, so we might as well, part of me thinks—
the wrong part, I know, the bad part, but still
let's pretend we're at that party where we met
and scandalized everyone, remember that part? Hold me
like that again, unbutton my shirt, part of you
wants to I can tell, I'm touching that part and it says
yes, the ardent partisan, let it win you over,
it's hopeless, come, we'll kiss and part forever.

note: *The sonnenizio was invented in Florence in the thirteenth century by
Vanni Fucci as an irreverent form whose subject was usually the impossibility
of everlasting love. Dante retaliated by putting Fucci into the seventh chasm of
the* Inferno *as a thief. Originally composed in hendecasyllabics, the sonnenizio
gradually moved away from metrical constraints and began to tackle a wider
variety of subject matter. The sonnenizio is fourteen lines long. It opens with a
line from someone else's sonnet, repeats a word from that line in each succeed-
ing line of the poem, and closes with a rhymed couplet.*

33

EX-BOYFRIENDS

They hang around, hitting on your friends
or else you never hear from them again.

They call when they're drunk, or finally get sober,

they're passing through town and want dinner,
they take your hand across the table, kiss you
when you come back from the bathroom.

They were your loves, your victims,
your good dogs or bad boys, and they're over

you now. One writes a book in which a woman

who sounds suspiciously like you
is the first to be sadistically dismembered
by a serial killer. They're getting married

and want you to be the first to know,
or they've been fired and need a loan,
their new girlfriend hates you,

they say they don't miss you but show up

in your dreams, calling to you from the shoeboxes

where they're buried in rows in your basement.

Some nights you find one floating into bed with you,

propped on an elbow, giving you a look

of fascination, a look that says *I can't believe*

I've found you. It's the same way

your current boyfriend gazed at you last night,

before he pulled the plug on the tiny white lights

above the bed, and moved against you in the dark

broken occasionally by the faint restless arcs

of headlights from the freeway's passing trucks,

the big rigs that travel and travel,

hauling their loads between cities, warehouses,

following the familiar routes of their loneliness.

DANCE

When you are finally, magically, able to clone
yourself into several identical women,

so that each one can move toward a man
who's been waiting for his turn

to come around for the first time, or maybe again,
won't you be happy then,

all of you together in a lustrous ballroom,
each woman wearing her distinguishing number,

the judges scoring everyone the same, music spilling
from the bandstand, the men thrilled

to be near you, each one whispering
a different pet name, each one polishing

with his black shoes a perfect circle of floor
while he raises you up, holding your

hips in his hands, gazing at you with his brown
or mottled green eyes, looking down

with his startling blue ones, taking you into a corner
then spinning you out toward the center

where the light from the mirrorball
splinters over your skin, sidereal

as your sequined dress, and you feel
as complete as you'll ever feel,

moving through all your true and beautiful lives
while the real one pales.

TWO

DEATH POEM

Do I have to bring it up again, isn't there another subject?
Can I forget about the scrap of flattened squirrel fur
fluttering on the road, can I forget the road
and how I can't stop driving no matter what,
not even for gas, or love, can I please not think
about my father left in some town behind me,
in his blue suit, with his folded hands,
and my grandmother moaning about her bladder
and swallowing all the pills, and the towns I'm passing now
can I try not to see them, the children squatting
by the ditches, the holes in their chests and foreheads,
the woman cradling her tumor, the dog dragging its crippled hips?
I can close my eyes and sit back if I want to,
I can lean against my friends' shoulders
and eat as they're eating, and drink from the bottle
being passed back and forth; I can lighten up, can't I,
Christ, can't I? There is another subject, in a minute
I'll think of it. I will. And if you know it, help me.
Help me. Remind me why I'm here.

SCARY MOVIES

Today the cloud shapes are terrifying,
and I keep expecting some enormous
black-and-white B-movie Cyclops
to appear at the edge of the horizon,

to come striding over the ocean
and drag me from my kitchen
to the deep cave that flickered
into my young brain one Saturday

at the Baronet Theater where I sat helpless
between my older brothers, pumped up
on candy and horror—that cave,
the litter of human bones

gnawed on and flung toward the entrance,
I can smell their stench as clearly
as the bacon fat from breakfast. This
is how it feels to lose it—

not sanity, I mean, but whatever it is
that helps you get up in the morning

and actually leave the house
on those days when it seems like death

in his brown uniform
is cruising his panel truck
of packages through your neighborhood.
I think of a friend's voice

on her answering machine—
Hi, I'm not here—
the morning of her funeral,
the calls filling up the tape

and the mail still arriving,
and I feel as afraid as I was
after all those vampire movies
when I'd come home and lie awake

all night, rigid in my bed,
unable to get up
even to pee because the undead
were waiting underneath it;

if I so much as stuck a bare
foot out there in the unprotected air
they'd grab me by the ankle and pull me
under. And my parents said there was

nothing there, when I was older
I would know better, and now
they're dead, and I'm older,
and I know better.

DEAD GIRLS

show up often in the movies, facedown
in the weeds beside the highway.
Kids find them by the river, or in the woods,

under leaves, one pink-nailed hand thrust up.
Detectives stand over them in studio apartments
or lift their photos off pianos

in the houses they almost grew up in.
A dead girl can kick a movie into gear
better than a saloon brawl, better

than a factory explosion, just
by lying there. Anyone can play her,
any child off the street

can be hog-tied and dumped from a van
or strangled blue in a kitchen, a bathroom,
an alley, a school. That's the beauty

of a dead girl. Even a plain one
who feels worthless
as a clod of dirt, broken

by the sorrow of gazing all day
at a fashion magazine,
can be made whole, redeemed

by what she finally can't help being,
the center of attention, the special,
desirable, dead, dead girl.

ECHO AND NARCISSUS

Poor love-struck Echo, stuck with repeating
everything he said. He might
have thought he deserved it,
to have a nymph for a girlfriend, who'd confirm
.

everything he said; he might
have loved how she mirrored him,
a girlfriend who'd say *You're pretty*
when he told her she was pretty,

who'd love him more than her mirror.
Not that they had mirrors in those days;
that was the problem. Anyway, she was pretty,
but he wasn't interested in nymphs.

If only they'd had mirrors in those days
he wouldn't have drowned in that reflecting pool,
finding it more interesting than nymphs.
But maybe he'd have hit his head against a mirror

if there'd been one instead of a pool, and died anyway.
No free will in those days—it was all the gods.

You could beat your head against your fate, but still,
if you were Narcissus, you'd end up a white flower

stuck in the ground with no will, plucked or trampled by
   gods,
and someone would say it was deserved,
for beauty to come down to a white flower,
a poor echo, and someone's love stuck

in the ground, the ground, the ground, the ground.

EATING TOGETHER

I know my friend is going,
though she still sits there
across from me in the restaurant,
and leans over the table to dip
her bread in the oil on my plate; I know
how thick her hair used to be,
and what it takes for her to discard
her man's cap partway through our meal,
to look straight at the young waiter
and smile when he asks
how we are liking it. She eats
as though starving—chicken, dolmata,
the buttery flakes of filo—
and what's killing her
eats, too. I watch her lift
a glistening black olive and peel
the meat from the pit, watch
her fine long fingers, and her face,
puffy from medication. She lowers
her eyes to the food, pretending
not to know what I know. She's going.
And we go on eating.

CAT POEM

The cat's hardly moving; she's stopped eating, stopped
     shitting, she puts her face to a bowl of water
but doesn't drink. My friend says not to write about her, he
     says no one wants to read about my pet
so let's say it's your cat, not mine, or maybe you have a dog;
     even I, a cat owner, think that dogs
are superior, they have such compassionate eyes. Once, an
     actor—not just any actor, but Al Pacino—
did an entire stage performance keeping in mind the liquid
     brown eyes of someone
in the audience, playing to those eyes, and when the house
     lights went up he realized
it was a guide dog, a German Shepherd, so maybe if you
     imagine your dog or even better
Al Pacino's dog, hardly moving, its ribs heaving, that would
     be preferable, but if you don't
like dogs maybe a bird will do, or whales, people seem to care
     about the whales, lying on their great sides
on the beach, or the seals with their skulls crushed by
     clubs—think of them, their orphaned pups—
or just forget about the animals entirely; forget the beagles
     smoking while they run on treadmills

and those rabbits the cosmetic companies seem to favor,
    though it's harder to discount
the chimpanzees injected with simian AIDS, unless maybe
    the retrovirus inhabiting your friend
has just become immune to the protease inhibitors, so forget
    the chimpanzees, too,
remember my cat? She's lying on the bathroom rug, her
    organs shutting down—imagine I wept
all day for her—Vanilla is her name, my daughter named her
    at five, now my daughter's grown,
now the cat's old, I've put her on the bed and I'm talking to
    her, saying It's all right,
go if you need to, and I'm watching death—he's stroking her
    fur, making his rounds,
he's talking to her softly, telling her to stop, ignoring me for
    now, ignoring you.

NOIR

Everybody dies, Bob Roberts, the crooked fight promoter,
tells Charlie Davis early in *Body and Soul*,
and it's the line Charlie throws back at him
like a perfect counterpunch at the close of the film.
The fix was in—go the distance and lose the decision—
but Charlie refused to take a dive,

thereby losing sixty grand but regaining his soul
and his long-suffering true love. *What're you gonna do,*
kill me? Everybody dies, Charlie says, and he
and his true love go laughing into the final frame.
In the alternate ending, written but never shot,
Charlie's killed and stuffed into a trashcan. What difference

if the audience leaves the theater believing
Charlie's still out there somewhere,
working a cash register like his mother
or teaching neighborhood kids the value
of a left hook to the ribs, an uppercut to the jaw?
Everybody dies. John Garfield, who played Charlie

and was notorious in Hollywood
for screwing all the starlets, died
in a hotel room at thirty-nine. My old father,
after a year of lying paralyzed
in a nursing home, finally died, allowing my mother
the relative relief of widowhood. Maybe Charlie

lived long enough to go the same way,
all those blows to the head
coming home to roost, while his true love
sat beside the bed, holding his useless hands
in hers. On the TV there'd be some forties movie
playing like a black-and-white memory,

full of torch songs and champagne
and money swirling down the screen
like rainwater down a drain. That night after the movie
a group of us dined on clams and salmon
and drank martinis in a noisy restaurant
whose neon sign might have read

Everybody Dies, since all of us would;
the waiters in their striped French T-shirts might even
have been there to ferry across to the other world anyone
    who did.
But it wasn't our time. We emerged intact
into an alley the rain was lacquering with a sheen
that seemed unreal, a movie set rain

orchestrated with levers and machinery
to suffuse the scene with the right proportion of melancholy
as we all stood a few minutes under a flickering light,
reluctant to part, the women buttoning their coats,
the men lowering the brims of their fedoras,
everybody finally dispersing into the night.

FEBRUARY 14

This is a valentine for the surgeons
ligating the portal veins and hepatic artery,
placing vascular clamps on the vena cava
as my brother receives a new liver.

And a valentine for each nurse;
though I don't know how many there are
leaning over him in their gauze masks,
I'm sure I have enough—as many hearts

as it takes, as much embarrassing sentiment
as anyone needs. One heart
for the sutures, one for the instruments
I don't know the names of,

and the monitors and lights,
and the gloves slippery with his blood
as the long hours pass,
as a T-tube is placed to drain the bile.

And one heart for the donor,
who never met my brother

but who understood the body as gift
and did not want to bury or burn that gift.

For that man, I can't imagine how
one heart could suffice. But I offer it.
While my brother lies sedated,
opened from sternum to groin,

I think of a dead man, being remembered
by others in their sorrow, and I offer him
these words of praise and gratitude,
oh beloved whom we did not know.

AND THEN I WOKE UP

What a relief to discover
that the doctor in my dream
did not exist, that his voice on the phone

and even the phone itself
were only figments, neural parcels
shipped from my brain stem

to my thalamus. And his news
about my grave illness was only
a synaptic frisson

deep in my cortex; I woke up
and was not dying. And my mother
was not slumped in the backseat

of a car she was supposed to be driving,
weeping, confused about where she lived.
But then, sadly, I had to realize

that the woman at the party
who told me, *Write faster*
and assured me of a prestigious literary prize

was also a chimera, as was the man
kissing me passionately under a tree—
its bright leaves evaporating

above our heads,
his tongue dissolving in my mouth
leaving only a gluey taste

I rinsed away with my coffee.
Already I'm forgetting what felt
like a great love, forgetting that world

which for the short while I lived there
had me fooled into believing
it was the only world; now

it is beginning to vanish,
along with everyone in it,
and this is their only elegy.

IN DREAMS

After eighteen years there's no real grief left
for the man who was my father.
I hardly think of him anymore,
and those dreams I used to have,

in which he'd be standing in a room of people
I didn't know—maybe his new friends,
if the dead have friendships—
those dreams no longer trouble my sleep.

He's not in the crooked houses I wander through
or in the field by the highway
where I'm running, chasing down
some important piece of paper,

desperate to reach it
as it's lifted in the wake of trucks
or flattened and marked by passing cars,
as it's lifted again to swirl over

a broken wood fence. I don't know why
the paper's so important, or if anything

is even written there.
I don't know where the dead go,

or why it's good to forget them,
not to see them if they come crowding
the windows or trying to lay themselves down
and press along our bodies at night

and ask that we love them again,
that our sorrows include them once more.
This morning I couldn't get up.
I slept late, I dreamed of the single

sheet of paper, which I never managed to reach
as it stuttered and soared over the grass
and a few flowers, so that I woke
with a sense of loss, wondering who

or what I had to mourn besides
my father, whom I no longer mourn,
father buried in the earth beneath grass,
beneath flowers I trample as I run.

THE WORK

I can't bear anymore what happens to the body,
how it begins to get ready, the skin drawing back
just slightly from the bones, the bones not
brittle yet but starting to abrade, the blood
slowing down in its thickening tunnels and sewers.
I don't want to see how the glossy hairs are leached
of their color, one strand at a time—
I think of how, after rain, ants get into the house,
how I first notice one or two veering toward
the dish sponge, then several behind the toaster
until I find a long line of them seething up
the pantry wall, pulsing on a jar lid, frantic
to get at the honey. What happens to
the sweet cave of the mouth, I don't want to see that.
Mottled roots of the cuspids exposed, the pocked
molars coming loose—lately I can't help noticing
how tired I look in the mornings, how ready
to return to the bed I've just risen from.
I make myself get dressed, I stand up and feel it
coming from beneath the earth, from the hulls

of their ribs and their weedy skulls, up through

the basement, the mildew and silverfish,

working steadily and humming, happy,

in love with its job of building an old woman.

FEVER BLUES

Maybe because I feel so dull and sick today,
the dozen harmonicas on my dresser,
snug in their gray plastic cases,
the lids popped open,

seem to me like little caskets I must caretake
before the arrival of the mourners—
a family named Hohner
which has suffered a grievous loss.

How similar death makes them—
the libidinous G, the guileless C,
even the strange D-flat.
They are tarnished where my lips

touched them, they have sung
while handling the snakes of sorrow,
happiness has knocked them down like a fit.
Now they are as quiet as unhitched boxcars

strewn in a train yard outside Chicago.
I've got the blues for everyone

who has to lie down like the dead all day,

far from the juke joint of health,

blues for the falling night

and the sheets wrung out from cancer, or fever,

the moonlit harps a flotilla

waiting to take us down to the mouth of the river.

WASHING

I haul my mother up from the tub,
my dripping, naked, trembling mother,

and help her onto the toilet lid where I used to sit
as a child, keeping her company

while she bathed, the delicate steam rising,
her breasts falling to each side,

the thick blonde hairs on her pubis
drifting like eelgrass, her belly as milky

as the swirls of soap on the surface of the water.
I sit her down and wrap her in a towel

and kneel to clip the curled yellow toenails,
taking each foot in my hands,

trying to be gentle, trying to be more merciful
than God, who after creating her

licked her clean with a rough tongue before
leaving her to her life, to suffering, and to me.

THREE

IT

I can still remember that sensation of being shaken
by something that gripped me and wouldn't let go
until my daughter was born, sliding toward the blanket
spread on the floor where I squatted,
the doctor squatting, too, waiting to catch her,
until she was completely outside of me
and the creature—thing—that had held me helpless
simply dropped me and turned away,
as though I were no longer interesting to it,
or tasted bad, as though suddenly remembering
urgent business elsewhere. And I felt I was again
the agent of my life; it was mine, and the new life
laid on my stomach after I'd staggered to the bed
was mine, too, I would have to learn
what she needed and how not to harm her.
But how could I protect her
from whatever had mastered me so completely,
opening my body ruthlessly to bring her down
into this world, how could I keep her
from that thing if it wanted to unmake her?
That morning of her birth I felt it close to me,

forcing out the sweat and screams, and I knew
it would have killed me if it had to, for her sake,
for those few hours it loved her
like a mother, as it had once loved me in order to get me out.

KNOWLEDGE

Even when you know what people are capable of,
even when you pride yourself on knowing,
on not evading history, or the news,
or any of the quotidian, minor, but still endlessly apparent
and relevant examples of human cruelty—even now
there are times it strikes you anew, as though
you'd spent your whole life believing that humanity
was fundamentally good, as though you'd never thought,
like Schopenhauer, that it was all blind, impersonal will,
never chanted perversely, almost gleefully,
the clear-sighted adjectives learned from Hobbes—
solitary, poor, nasty, brutal, and short—
even now you're sometimes stunned to hear
of some terrible act that sends you reeling off, too overwhelmed
even to weep, and then you realize that your innocence,
which you had thought no longer existed,
did, in fact, exist—that somewhere underneath your cynicism
you still held out hope. But that hope has been shattered now,
irreparably, or so it seems, and you have to go on, afraid
that there is more to know, that one day you will know it.

CALIFORNIA STREET

The two drunks have staked out a spot on the steep sidewalk,
   backs to the brick wall,
one thrusting his legs out so that pedestrians have to round a
   parking meter to avoid them,
the other curled with his head in the first man's lap, beside
   them two pint bottles,
obviously empty now since otherwise the one still upright
   would be drinking, and not
looking balefully at each person passing, as though he'd
   asked for money and they'd refused
to give him anything—though in fact he hasn't asked, unless
   you consider that his presence itself,
his stained pants and filthy Levi's jacket, the long tangle of
   graying beard, the stink rising from both of them
as he strokes the black hair of his passed-out friend, is a kind
   of asking, which won't be answered
by us, making our way past them up the hill, who give them
   a brief look and then let them go.

THE WAY OF THE WORLD

We know the ugly hate the beautiful,
and the bitter losers are all seething
over bad coffee, washed in the sleazy fluorescence
of fast-food restaurants. We know

the wheelchairs hate the shoes,
and the medicines envy the vitamins,
which is why sometimes a whole bottle
of sleeping pills will gather like a wave

and rush down someone's throat to drown
in the sour ocean of the stomach.
And let's not even mention the poor,
since hardly anyone does.

It's the way of the world—
the sorrowful versus the happy,
and the stupid against everyone,
especially themselves. So don't pretend

you're glad when your old friends
get lucky in work, or love,

while you're still drifting through life
like a lobster in a restaurant tank. Go on,

admit it: you'd claw them to death
if you could. But you're helpless,
knocking futiley against clear glass you can't
break through. They're opening champagne,

oblivious of you, just as you don't notice
how many backs you've scrambled over
to get this far, your black eyes glittering,
your slow limbs grimly and steadily working.

DEAR SIR OR MADAM

This letter is the one you shouldn't open.
Or if you have, please don't read further.
It is going to give you terrible news.

Oh sir, or madam, we are strangers
but forgive me, I feel as though I love you
typing this on the forty-seventh floor

alone except for the man who cleans the carpets.
Forgive me if I grow distracted,
and think of my own burdens . . .

a wife's ashes, a boy who rocks back and forth
all day, and babbles nonsense. His photograph
and hers are on my desk; he doesn't smile.

The doctors test and test, then send
him to another. Maybe you, sir, or madam,
have felt a kind of helplessness at how things go?

I'm trying to finish this, to tell you
what I'm paid to tell you,
what I have stayed here late to compose

in just the right fashion, even if it takes
all night—the janitor has gone,
turning off all the lights. There's only my lamp,

and the quiet. . . . My wife liked quiet. She liked
to hold me without either of us talking,
just breathing together. Sir,

breathe with me now. Madam, hold on to me.
There is news I must give you.
Let's not speak of it yet.

ONE NATION UNDER GOD

Certain parts of your body,
don't you just want
to cut them off, they're so disgusting?
Don't you wish you could plane away

your ass, your thighs, half your nose,
until you looked *right*?

And people who don't get your jokes
or literary references, I mean
when you deliver the perfect line
from A *Streetcar Named Desire*

that absolutely fits the occasion
and your companion only looks
at you blankly—you want

to strangle him, don't you?
Just take his tie—
people who wear ties
deserve what they get—
and loop it around his neck

the way a junkie takes a thin
rubber tube and squeezes it

around the arm so the veins pop?
Can't we rid ourselves of junkies
while we're at it, shoot them full

of that contaminated heroin from Mexico
that eats through flesh?
All the blacks and Italians, the Asians

and natural blondes,
wouldn't it be better to round them up
and ship them all someplace

like Texas and surround them
with a big electric fence,

and don't try to tell me that a redwood
or a zygote or a lever-pulling monkey

in a lab is more important
than a human being, because then

I'm going to want to fuck you up really bad.
Reckless freeway drivers, I know
we're on the same page there.

Lane-changers, tailgaters, swervy
Indy 500 wanna-bes, they should just
be lined up and shot, execution-style.

And speaking of executions. How many
have there been lately? Not nearly enough.

We've got problems in this country I tell you.
If thy right eye offend thee
you know what to do.
And thy left eye, too.

CHICKEN

Why did she cross the road?
She should have stayed in her little cage,
shat upon by her sisters above her,
shitting on her sisters below her.

God knows how she got out.
God sees everything. God has his eye
on the chicken, making her break
like the convict headed for the river,

sloshing his way through the water
to throw off the dogs, raising
his arms to starlight to praise
whatever isn't locked in a cell.

He'll make it to a farmhouse
where kind people will feed him.
They'll bring green beans and bread,
home-brewed hops. They'll bring

the chicken the farmer found
by the side of the road, dazed

from being clipped by a pickup,
whose delicate brain stem

he snapped with a twist,
whose asshole his wife stuffed
with rosemary and a lemon wedge.
Everything has its fate,

but only God knows what that is.
The spirit of the chicken will enter the convict.
Sometimes, in his boxy apartment,
listening to his neighbors above him,

annoying his neighbors below him,
he'll feel a terrible hunger
and an overwhelming urge
to jab his head at the television over and over.

MISSING BOY BLUES

I'm lying in a field, hope you find me pretty soon.
Lying in a field, hope you find me pretty soon.
I'm afraid of being nothing but a few old bones.

If I think of my name, then maybe you'll hear it.
If I think of my name then maybe you'll hear.
Grass blade. Crow eye. Crushed berry. Worm in the dirt.

In science we had a life-sized skeleton.
It hung in the classroom all year long.
It hung by the blackboard, all alone. . . .

Sacrum, parietal, metacarpal bone.
I failed the test, got too many answers wrong.

Once I asked my mother if God was all over.
I asked if He saw us. I had a high fever—
She said she didn't know, and straightened my covers.

Then she kissed my face; then she kissed my hair.
(Then he tore my pajamas and my legs were bare.)
If you're still looking for me, you won't find me anywhere.

HUMAN NATURE

When I hear of how he kept one girl alive
after disposing of the friend and mother,
and about the next one he found

and killed and cut apart,
I try to imagine him hooking his fingers
through the plastic rings of a six-pack,

lifting a nozzle from its cradle
to gas up a truck, flicking
the dead end of a cigarette into the weeds,

and I don't want him to be human—
shaking water from a comb,
jiggling the handle of a toilet, fishing

for a quarter to drop into the slot
of a meter. I want him tentacled
and eyeless, like some

creature from a star so far away
it's not charted anywhere, its light
stopping short of earth.

I want him to be a shapeless
lump of matter that is not
our matter, not carbon-based,

maybe I don't even want him
to be alive—silicon, circuitry,
inert mass of material. Then

he'd be no more capable of evil
than a rock or stick—rock brought down
hard on a skull, stick whittled

to a fine point and tipped with poison—
there still would be someone,
a god to work the levers, to set him

in motion. Better not to think
of a god like that, better to believe
there's nothing; nothing, and the human.

FOUR

LUSH LIFE

In this bottle a searing headache,
in that one a car angling off the road
to meet a tree in your neighbor's yard,

in the next one a man who removes
your clothes while you spin
down into the whirlpool of the bed's black sheets.

At the bottom of another: locked metal box
you can't pry open, though you can hear
someone in there, muttering and crying

and saying how sorry she is.
And don't forget the worm of shame
that uncurls in your throat sometimes,

and the bathrooms where you crouched
shaking before a toilet, your hair limp,
the sour evening rising up inside you.

So what are you doing, sitting there
holding a half-full highball glass,
listening to the jazz of ice, the slow blues

of a just-lit cigarette? Some low voice
is crooning your name, and in the double
being poured behind the bar

the tenor sax is starting its solo, taking you
out over the changes, sounding
just like love, just like it won't ever stop.

BAD GIRL

She's the one sleeping all day, in a room
at the back of your brain. She wakes up
at the sound of a cork twisted free
of a bottle, a stabbed olive

plopped into gin. She's prettier than you
and right now you bore the shit out of her,
sitting there sipping when she wants
to stand on the rim of the glass, naked,

dive straight to the bottom and lie there
looking up, amazed at how the world
wavers and then comes clear. You're not
going to let her. You've locked her in

with her perfume and cheap novels,
her deep need for trouble. She's the one
calling to you through the keyhole,
then sneaking away to squirm out

a window and tear her silk dress.
You can't guess where she's going,

or who you'll wake up with
when you finally wake up,

your head throbbing like a heart.
She's the one you're scared of,
the one who dares you to go ahead
and completely disappear. It's not

you the boys are noticing, not you
turning toward them and throwing off light.
You're crouched in a corner, coming undone.
She's in love with you now. She's the one.

'ROUND MIDNIGHT

In the book I'm reading: hard rain,
spike heels on pavement,
a man waiting in a rented room

to draw a woman down onto his bed.
She's the wrong woman,
she's a car wreck in a silk dress

and he can't wait to touch her.
No plot without desire,
the more desperate the better.

I look up to find that here, too,
it's raining. And now that I'm back
in my own quiet life

I feel like a character who's barely
been imagined yet, just a name
wearing a faded T-shirt,

reaching for her glass of cold wine.

If only the river would surge into the streets,

if only a tree would uproot itself

or the roof fly off in a funnel of black wind.

Such is my life: A minute ago I was happy,

immersed in a book. Now I feel a misery

only violence could cure. Now

I have to invent a story

to drag me out into the city,

toward music and grainy light

and the wrong men, I have to discover

what it is I want

and who I'm going to have to hurt to get it.

SOUTH OF THE BORDER

Here by the pool in Rosarito
we are playing Lotería

with handfuls of pale, freckled beans,
placing them on cards with illustrations:

the dead man, the drunk man, the spider,
the bat. We are alive, unfortunately sober

after several weak margaritas,
and there is no spider here to bite us

and nothing to swoop down, hideous-faced and black-
winged, to harvest us like hapless gnats;

the troubles are all elsewhere,
and frankly we don't really care;

we are lining up our beans, ordering
shots of tequila to strengthen our drinks

and we are going to get good and fucked up
and lie like the dead on our chaise lounges, happy

to be lucky, lying row after burning row
here by the pool in Rosarito.

BODY AND SOUL

Where do you think the soul is?
Do you think it looks like a small paper bag,

the kind that contains one item—
candy bar, liquid soap, pint bottle?

Is it crumpled up behind the heart?
Is it folded neatly, wedged between the ribs,

is it wrapped around the balls, is it damp
like a cunt, has it been torn?

The body isn't the house.
If the body is the house,

is the soul up late in the kitchen, sleepless,
standing before the open refrigerator,

is it tired of TV,
sickened by its own thoughts?

The body has no thoughts.
The body soaks up love like a paper towel

and is still dry.
The body shoots up some drugs,

sweats and weeps—
Sometimes the body

gets so quiet
it can hear the soul,

scratching like something trapped
inside the walls

and trying frantically
to get out.

BLUES FOR ROBERT JOHNSON

Give me a pint of whiskey with a broken seal
Give me one more hour with a broken feel
I can't sleep again and a black dog's on my trail

You're singing hell hound, crossroad, love in vain
You're singing, and the black sky is playing rain
You're stomping your feet, shaking the windowpane

I put my palm to the glass to get the cold
I drink the memories that scald
Drink to the loves that failed and failed

Look down into the river, I can see you there
Looking down into the blue light of a woman's hair
Saying to her *Baby, dark gon' catch me here*

You're buried in Mississippi under a stone
You're buried and still singing under the ground
And the blues fell mama's child, tore me all upside down

THIS POEM WANTS TO BE A ROCK
AND ROLL SONG SO BAD

I'm gathered with my friends in my parents' garage
between the Toro mower and the washer,
practicing this poem at a deafening volume
while inhaling non-stick Pam from a Ziploc.

This poem captures the essence of today's youth,
a raunchy perfume named Fuck It,
excreted from the balls of a civet.

I like how those lines rhyme, just like in a song.
Tupac Shahid Anne Sexton Erica Jong.

Let me tell you what this poem really wants:
it wants to make you slam dance and fist pump
until you crawl across a sticky club floor,
weeping with profound understanding

before you vomit in the Women's Room sink.
It wants you to listen to it over and over and over
so that thirty years from now

whatever wayward idiocy you were up to
will come back glazed with nostalgia—

Gee, remember wandering around the golf course
hallucinating in the middle of the night,
remember the security guard at your dad's work
finding us naked, and that guy with the knife
convinced we were insects from outer space,

those were the days, and that poem
was on everybody's car radio, in heavy rotation.
Let's go get the book again

and feel like we used to. Light some incense,
and a bunch of those little vanilla votives.
Come over here and ravish me

while I recite this poem word for word,
including the awesome guitar solo
I can play with this beautiful instrument
made out of nothing but air.

BUGDOM

Sometimes, in a certain mood, I feel bad I haven't died yet
and I'm jealous of the people who have, the ones everyone
    remembers
    and fetishizes just because they're dead. It's the way I feel
when the phone down the hall rings for someone else

and I realize I will spend Friday night in an exotic European
    capital
alone in my room, playing a computer game called Bugdom
    in which a little striped beetle wanders through the electronic
    grass
trying to avoid banana slugs with bulging eyes

    while kicking open walnuts for magic shamrocks and strawberries.
I start to regret missing all those opportunities to die young,
    to be remembered as I was at seventeen, at twenty-five, at
    thirty-two.
I'm sorry I never overdosed, those years doing heroin, and that I
    managed

to free climb the cliffs above the river without falling, that
        later I survived
the earthquake that collapsed the bridge, clinging to the wall
        in a friend's house; I watched her best-selling books
pitch off the shelves, then went on living quietly, growing older

        and less interesting every year. Let me tell you about
                Bugdom, a game
that won't let you rest: soon the enormous spear-wielding red ants
        begin appearing, and if one nails you, you sit down, defeated,
before you've got to right yourself again and run blindly

        in every direction while they chase you, all the while avoiding
the more and more numerous slugs, and searching for the walnuts
        that will finally give you a red or orange key so you can enter
a new, more beautiful landscape of sunflowers

        filled with flying insects in boxing gloves trying to punch your
                lights out.
Next you have to swim up a river while the ants heave stones
        to try and crush you, and after that, it feels like everything
comes at you at once, and if it weren't for those walnuts

you think you'd probably just sit down and let the slugs
slime through you, the ants stab you again and again, and the
    insects
        knock you down for the count. So alone in this city, and far
from the few people who, unbelievably, love me, I focus

        on what will get me through—the pretty flowered sheets
on my single bed, cold leftovers and wine, the inane
        and relentlessly hopeful music that accompanies the bug as it
            struggles up
a steep slope and stops, panting, the hero of its tiny, challenged life.

THIS POEM IS IN RECOVERY

If you think I'm going to raise one single frosted martini glass
or a rocks tumbler in whose liquid the reflection
and noise of a pinball machine trembles, *chink-kachink-ka-ka-ka-
    chink,*

or even a little Herradura shot glass from Mexico
or a goblet etched with the name of a winery
and a rearing horse, if you think a green or amber bottle

is going to make an appearance, or you're holding out
for a can of Mickeys Big Mouth or hopefully a charming leather
    flask,
forget you. I'm not even going to reminisce about all the vodka—

drink of a tragic people—that I consumed beside the Neva,
watching the drawbridges ratchet up and down
and the elaborate fountains at the czar's palace foam

like the champagne my new husband shook and let explode
all over us, or—forget me—I won't even hold forth
on the Victorians' justified condemnation of gin

(mothers abandoning their newborns in gutters, etc.)
or the large numbers of pifflicated Japanese monks
gazing syllabically at the moon or the river of blossoms.

I'm going to forgo my usual subject matter, along with much
of history and literature, in favor of the present,
absolutely alcohol-free moment. Here it is:

Here it is again:
I'm not going to get drunk and take off my clothes
to sign my book for you, or bite you on the mouth

in a bathroom with the light off so it's as black in there
as an entire case of Freixenet bottles
while the raucous party goes on in the hotel suite.

And I am definitely not going to climb the stoplight
or fall through the sliding glass doors
or try to pole dance on the stripper's night off.

None of that nonsense here. Here we're all recovering.
Chamomile, or lemon? Plain or sparkling?
How about decaf? Here comes another moment

attached to nothing. Here comes too much
peace and quiet, while we wait for our demons
to shake off their hangovers and pay us a visit.

FIVE

DEAR READER

Tonight I am amazed by all the people making love
while I sit alone in my pajamas in a foreign country
with my dinner of cookies and vodka. And I am amazed
that my own country still exists, though I am not in it
to speak its language or break its drug laws. How astonishing

to realize that I am not the glass being shattered
on the street below, or the laughter that follows it;
I'm not even one of the congregation on my small TV,
getting the Lord's good news, though I can reach
the screen by leaning forward, and touch

the wavering lines of each transfigured face. I tell you
I can't get over it sometimes, I still have trouble
believing that an egg deep inside my own body
went and turned into someone else, who right now
is on a tour boat on the river, having forgotten

how she used to hold on to my legs whenever I tried
to leave the room. Right now, somewhere I am not,
the history of the world is being decided,
and the terrible things I'd rather not think of
go on and on without stopping, while I separate

the two halves of another cookie and lick
the cream filling, and pour myself one more
and drink to you, dear reader, amazed
that you are somewhere in the world without me,
listening, trying to hold me in your hands.

ON KNOCKING OVER MY GLASS
WHILE READING SHARON OLDS

The milk spread,
a translucent stain
covering the word *milk*,

snaking down toward *come*
and *womb* and *penis*, toward *gashes*
and *swiveled*, toward the graceful

grey flower and the infelicitous
errless digit, so that suddenly
the page seemed to be weeping,

the way a statue of the Virgin
in some poor but devout parish
might begin to weep, ichor streaming

from the eyes, the open palms,
so that when the girl kneeling
in the rain of the convent yard

touches the mottled white
folds of the stone robe
her lupus disappears. And I felt

as that girl must have felt,
that the Holy Mother herself
had come to reveal

the true nature of the real,
goddess in the statue,
bread in each word's

black flowering, and I rose
and went to the kitchen—
sacristy of the cupboards,

tabernacle of the fridge—
to refill my glass
with her wild and holy blood.

FUCK

There are people who will tell you
that using the word *fuck* in a poem
indicates a serious lapse
of taste, or imagination,

or both. It's vulgar,
indecorous, an obscenity
that crashes down like an anvil
falling through a skylight

to land on a restaurant table,
on the white linen, the cut-glass vase of lilacs.
But if you were sitting
over coffee when the metal

hit your saucer like a missile,
wouldn't that be the first thing
you'd say? Wouldn't you leap back
shouting, or at least thinking it,

over and over, bell-note riotously clanging
in the church of your brain

while the solicitous waiter
led you away, wouldn't you prop

your shaking elbows on the bar
and order your first drink in months,
telling yourself you were lucky
to be alive? And if you wouldn't

say anything but *Mercy* or *Oh my*
or *Land sakes,* well then
I don't want to know you anyway
and I don't give a fuck what you think

of my poem. The world is divided
into those whose opinions matter
and those who will never have
a clue, and if you knew

which one you were I could talk
to you, and tell you that sometimes
there's only one word that means
what you need it to mean, the way

there's only one person
when you first fall in love,
or one infant's cry that calls forth
the burning milk, one name

that you pray to when prayer
is what's left to you. I'm saying
in the beginning was the word
and it was good, it meant one human

entering another and it's still
what I love, the word made
flesh. *Fuck me*, I say to the one
whose lovely body I want close,

and as we fuck I know it's holy,
a psalm, a hymn, a hammer
ringing down on an anvil,
forging a whole new world.

AUGURY

That girl in the stilettos and tight dress
    is my girl, parading back and forth
        before my closet

in the precarious shoes she bought for the prom.
    She thinks she has to practice being sexy. She can't
        imagine the future

I can see so clearly: over the calm sea
    of the mirror, a thousand warriors set out,
        ready to kill

or die for the sake of her beauty.
    I can see how the tiny sails will disappear
        into the distance,

looking like they're going under, swallowed
    by some jealous god or other. She stares intently
        at the mirror

but still she can't see the ships foundering,
      the hearts being dashed on the rocks. Now
           she smoothes glittery

shadow over her eyelids, dark lipstick
      on her mouth. When she blows a kiss
           a wind drags

the waves up to a great height, before
      they topple over and crush any man
           who's still alive.

PROVERBIAL

The birds are up early; it's rush hour on the lawn,
and cars fly over the bridges and into the city
in spite of the burnings. I know the true worth
of the sayings my grandmother served up with the lasagna.
My grandmother saw the trees, as did my mother. Father
was alone in the forest. Meanwhile, we children
were raised by wolves; two wrongs
don't make a right are the directions to my house.
But even the blind chicken finds
the kernel of corn, even the unhatched eggs
wobble in their basket and promise
to one day explode into swans,
however modest or far away.

CEILING

As a kid, I used to pretend
          to walk on the ceilings of my parents' house;
     I'd hold a mirror like a plate, or a tray,
the way I'd use it later

to snort a line of coke off of.
          But before I discovered more sophisticated ways
     of making the world disappear,
I'd go from room to room

looking down into the mirror,
          stepping carefully over doorjambs
     and around light fixtures,
happy as the flies that crawled up there,

or as happy as I imagined flies
          must be, though really who knew about them,
     they always sounded so angry
with their tiny buzz saw voices—

In the real house, my oldest brother
          would be trying to slam my father into a doorway

or chasing his siblings
around the table with a butcher knife;

he'd pull me out of hiding in a closet
        to practice hitting something weaker. No wonder
    . I wanted to live on the pure white ceiling
and inhale the clean granules that turned

my brain starry, no wonder I envied
        the flies, caroming above us, or tracking through sugar
        and careening out the open screen door
though sometimes someone picked up a swatter

and smacked them dead against
        the window glass—a fate I also occasionally envied—
        but now I'm glad I'm here,
years and miles from my handsome, troubled family,

on vacation next to a shimmering lagoon
        with egrets wading into their serene reflections
        and workmen on the roof next door
hammering and sawing, the sound of repair going on all day.

CONVERSATION

This is a paean to last night's dinner conversation,
which began with a discussion
of the transportive virtues of various wines
before my friend and I set out on our expedition

over vast territories of subject matter,
as if we were the early explorers of America,
charting the scarification practices
of Bay Area tribes, mapping the terrain

between carcinoma and rare books,
preparing our report for the faraway king:
the forests of literary influence,
the arroyos of rehab and elevator sex,

the great prairies of Zoloft and home ownership.
Over dessert, our talk at last arrived
at the legendary cities of gold,
the five photographs of Marilyn Monroe

reputed to grace the wall of the Men's Room
at Tosca's in North Beach. Reader, I am here

to assure you of the truth of this account.
We headed down Columbus, past Kerouac Alley,

the conversation leading to the act itself
the way talking about, say, kissing someone
can lead, if you're lucky, to a cessation
of all conversation—and as I stood before the three

porcelain urinals, and beheld her true loveliness,
I knew I had to deliver this image to you,
so that you might suddenly feel the urge
to talk your way into a daring adventure,

like circumnavigating the globe
or the rooms of your house, or your own heart,
which has never stopped wanting to tell you
what journeys are yet to be taken.

ROMANCE

Remember how you waited for your first French kiss,
    that exotic term for what turned out to be the shock
of an oily eel entering your mouth;
    remember a boy's arm flung over your shoulder,

his sweaty hand inching down your blouse
    like a snail moving toward a cabbage leaf,
remember being finger-fucked in some house under construction
    and the kid who spied on you masturbating in your bedroom

and how you grew up believing anyway that romance
    was going to tuck you under its tender white wing
and carry you off to someplace where you'd never notice
    all the flies getting married to the corpses

of bloated deer and raccoons by the roadside,
    or the man outside the corner store, engaged
to every dusty bottle on the shelf, or the penned cows
    yearning for the hammer to the skull, for something certain;

still here you are, in middle age, stunned
    to find yourself in a sushi bar in California

with a man kneeling before you
    while the little wooden sampans drift past

with their cargoes of dead tuna and seaweed,
    and he is not asking you for anything
but to stay exactly where you are, to please not disappear
    while he goes to feed the parking meter,

and the man behind the counter is nodding and smiling,
    raising his cleaver aloft and taking aim
and letting it fall
    sharp and precise on the glistening bodies of fish.

MINIATURES

I love those vodka bottles on the plane
you can line up on your tray table,
and the miniature blackberry preserves
in the boutique hotel, where in the bathroom

there are little soaps and lotions, a sewing kit
with enough thread for one button, a needle
with an eye so tiny it's invisible. Once in a museum
I saw sculptures that required a microscope

to make out the three birds perched
on a single filament of hair; the artist worked,
it was said, between heartbeats, because the pulse
in his thumb could ruin everything. I love

that there's a realm in which we're giants,
crashing through the shrubs and sending
the lizards skittering, scattering the methodical ants
who toil toward the rotted log with leaves

twice their size. I love not looking up
into the measureless black fathoms

of space, which only make me think
of the enormous darkness of the future

no matter what the scientists say
about all that past light streaming in.
Years ago, I built a dollhouse
for my daughter, from a kit. It took

months of fitful work, but finally
I glued the last wood chip to the roof,
set the furniture in place,
and we moved the family in. I loved

to watch Dad peeing in the kitchen
and Mom dancing in the clawfoot tub
while Baby somersaulted up the stairs.
At night, when they and my daughter

had been tucked into bed, I loved
to stand over them,
listening to the house settle,
looking down into the world

I had made, and could save.

KISSES

All the kisses I've ever been given, today I feel them on my
    mouth.
And my knees feel them, the reckless ones placed there
through the holes in my jeans while I sat on a car hood
or a broken sofa in somebody's basement, stoned, the way I
    was
in those days, still amazed that boys and even men would
    want to
lower their beautiful heads like horses drinking from a river
    and taste me.
The back of my neck feels them, my hair swept aside to
    expose the nape,
and my breasts tingle the way they did when my milk came in
    after the birth,
when I was swollen, and sleepless, and my daughter fed and
    fed until I pried
her from me and laid her in her crib. Even the chaste kisses
    that brushed
my cheeks, the fatherly ones on my forehead, I feel them
    rising up from underneath
the skin of the past, a delicate, roseate rash; and the ravishing
    ones, God,

I think of them and the filaments in my brain start buzzing
crazily and flare out.

Every kiss is here somewhere, all over me like a fine, shiny
grit, like I'm a pale

fish that's been dipped in a thick swirl of raw egg and
dragged through flour,

slid down into a deep skillet, into burning. Today I know I've
lost no one.

My loves are here: wrists, eyelids, damp toes, all scars, and
my mouth

pouring praises, still asking, saying *kiss me*; when I'm dead
kiss this poem,

it needs you to know it goes on, give it your lovely mouth,
your living tongue.